COMPLETE

TRASH

COMPLETE
TRASH

THE BEST WAY TO GET RID OF PRACTICALLY EVERYTHING AROUND THE HOUSE

NORM CRAMPTON

M. EVANS AND COMPANY   NEW YORK

Library of Congress Cataloging-in-Publication Data

Crampton, Norman.
    Complete trash : the best way to get rid of practically everything
around the house / Norm Crampton.
        p. cm.
    ISBN 0-87131-572-6
    1. House cleaning. 2. Commercial products—Recycling. 3. Refuse
and refuse disposal. I. Title.
TX324.C72 1989   89-1516   648—dc20

M. Evans and Company, Inc.
216 East 49 Street
New York, New York 10017

Illustrations by Daniel J. Hochstatter

Design by Manuela Paul

Manufactured in the United States of America

Quoted material on page 43 from *Washington Goes to War*, by David Brinkley. Copyright © 1988 by David Brinkley. Reprinted by permission of Alfred
A. Knopf, Inc.   Material on page 57 from *Hazardous Wastes from Homes*
(Santa Monica, CA; Enterprise for Education, Inc., 1988). Reprinted by
permission of the publisher.

INTRODUCTION
Just Talking to Myself

*I*t's getting harder to throw things away, and for anyone who enjoys disposal as much as I do, that is not good news. Since childhood I have always liked to take the garbage out. Other kids complained about this chore. For me it was pleasure. Getting rid of things—tossing, junking, cleaning the decks—has always given me a deep satisfaction that stops just this side of compulsion. I have thought about this behavior and concluded it fits right into my personality. Disposal is the handmaiden of an orderly mind, and I am orderly. Others may preserve order by squirreling things away, stuffing their attics and cellars full of old appliances, discredited theses, tarnished icons, and sundry household props. I prefer to put them at the curb. Next to the garbage.

I live with my family in a Midwestern suburb where it is still possible to dispose of anything simply by putting it out for the Wednesday garbage pickup. "Anything" may be an overstatement. I haven't tried everything. But I have put out small trees, leaking water heaters, defunct lawn mowers, and, of course, the endless tons of more commonplace trash: bags and bags of grass and leaves; newspapers and magazines, many barely skimmed; stacks of junk mail; bales of beer and soda bottles; and even some garbage. The amazing part, when you consider inflation and the cost of things, is that my garbageman takes it all away without complaint for the grand sum of eleven dollars a month. I consider that an incredible bargain—it's practically free.

And I know this can't last forever. The first warning arrived in the mail the other day. Stapled to my garbage bill was a little "Dear Customer" note explaining that service charges were going up to twelve dollars a month immediately. The reason, my garbageman explained, was "stricter EPA standards, coupled with new state and local taxes on final disposal." I don't mind paying a dollar a month more, but I have a feeling this is only the first shot in an assault on my constitutional right to keep and bear trash.

Reports are coming in from other parts of the country, and they are not encouraging. In a growing number of towns my preferred method of disposal—helter-skelter—is no longer acceptable. Law-abiding citizens are being told to separate their trash: bottles here, cans there, paper in a separate stack. States are issuing trash decrees. New Jersey prohibits grass and leaves in the landfill. Florida has practically outlawed my favorite plastic invention, the six-pack connector. Minnesota has declared that car batteries cannot be thrown out, period. What's going on?

I know what you're going to say, and you're right—there really is a waste-disposal crisis out there. Yes, some town dumps are full to the brim. Some are contaminating the water supply. Yes, incinerating trash causes problems unless it is very carefully managed. Yes, recycling and composting are not operating anywhere near capacity. Yes, that's all true, but it's unrelated to my immediate need, which is to get rid of this overstuffed bag of trash. Lacking any better response to my problem, the authorities have decided to change human nature. I know it's just a matter of time until the trash traditions at our house will have to change. But not too fast—I need to talk myself into the new way to dispose.

This book is a collection of sermonettes on household trash, arranged alphabetically and suitable for reading aloud. The goal of each short piece is to arrive at a "best way" to dispose of that particular item. "Best" is a judgment based on what well-informed people are saying about such things as: what happens to trash after it is buried or burned; how much are we throwing away of various things; how much room do we have in the various disposal channels; and other parts of the disposal dialogue. Though this is not a technical book, you'll find facts and figures, just enough to catch attention or to make a case. Remember, I'm trying to sell myself on these ideas, too.

You'll find a variety of recommended disposal methods, whatever seems appropriate, all things considered. Experts say our national goal is not to quit using any present disposal method but to adjust the mix. As a nation, we're burying too much trash—80% at least. Landfill space is growing scarce and expensive in many communities— that's why my garbage bill is going up. Meanwhile we're skittish about burning wastes to recover heat, and we're only beginning to catch on to recycling. Both disposal methods deserve much wider use.

Finally, one all-purpose disclaimer. The views and recommendations expressed here are my own, based on the best available information. I hope this book helps you to dispose of household wastes in the best way possible in your neighborhood. In all cases, the last word on any waste-disposal question belongs to your local government professionals. This is a friendly way of saying that neither the author nor the publisher is liable for any injury, humiliation, or public scorn you may suffer as a result of following the advice in *Complete Trash*. We'll take full credit, however, for the personal satisfaction you gain in changing your disposal habits.

Ready . . . set . . . dispose!

—Norm Crampton
Flossmoor, Illinois

ALUMINUM CANS

*M*om, apple pie, and recycled aluminum cans—you can't get much more American. Is there a Scout Troop, Ladies' Aid, or Neighborhood Improvement Society that does not know the virtue of recycling aluminum cans? Virtue is not their only reward. Aluminum beer and soda cans are worth about half a cent each at the recycler—40 to 50 cents a pound. If those numbers fail to excite interest, consider this: Half of the cans in the six pack you load in your shopping cart today were somebody's discards less than two months ago. The typical empty can is remelted and back on the store shelf within six weeks. That's almost metaphysical.

The aluminum industry reports that more than 50% of all cans now are recycled. During twenty years of recycling programs, the industry says it has paid $3.57 billion for 275 billion used cans. Aluminum recycling is such a raging success that it has raised the question: Why not do the same with glass, plastic, and steel containers? But the model doesn't fit. The most important difference is that aluminum has a much higher market value than glass, steel, or plastic. While aluminum fetches 45 cents a pound, glass brings just 2 cents. Plastic beverage bottles earn more than glass as scrap but operate under a unique recycling

handicap: Federal law says plastic food containers must be made of virgin materials, not remelted ones. So the recycling loop doesn't neatly close with plastic as it does with aluminum and glass.

As for steel cans, their share of the beverage container market versus aluminum has plummeted from near 100% three decades ago to about 5% today. The steel industry would like to turn those numbers around again, but the odds are long. Aluminum conquered the market with a seamless, lighter can, reducing leakage and transportation costs. Recycling added to these advantages—aluminum made from recycled cans requires only 5% of the electric power needed to extract the metal from virgin bauxite ore. Thus the aluminum industry has found it advantageous to promote recycling and keep the stream of old cans flowing in. By supporting recycling, the beverage industry also has defended itself against criticism that it creates litter. The industry has defeated bottle- and can-deposit laws by acting like a good corporate citizen.

Best way to get rid of aluminum cans: Recycle them—there is no other sensible option. If you don't want to tote them to a recycler, find some activist in your neighborhood or building who will take them off your hands. Let virtue be its own reward.

AMMONIA AND AMMONIA-BASED CLEANERS

*P*eople who have ammonia and ammonia-based cleaners to dispose of apparently have quit cleaning—run out of elbow grease, so to speak. But we'll not examine their motives any further. The answer, please!

Best way to get rid of ammonia and ammonia-based cleaners: Use up whatever liquid remains (sorry, you'll just have to scrub some more), rinse the container with water, and toss in the trash.

Warning: Never mix ammonia with chlorine bleach. Some people have done this thinking they would get a more powerful cleaning agent. Instead, what they get is a deadly gas and—ironically—a liquid that has virtually no cleaning power compared to the separate chemicals.

ANTIFREEZE

We prefer to leave car-radiator chores to our service station. But enough other people handle antifreeze at home that proper disposal has become an issue. Opinion is divided. Some experts say antifreeze should be treated as a hazardous waste. Others say it's okay to flush antifreeze down the drain—that the toxic ethylene glycol it contains will be safely treated at the sewage plant. We'll take this second option.

Best way to get rid of antifreeze: Flush it down the toilet. Never ever pour it on the ground. Antifreeze has a sweet taste attractive to pets, and it's lethal.

Appliances, Large

If you want to sound like an expert on trash, speak of large household appliances the way professionals do. Call them "white goods" (because the majority are white). Stoves, refrigerators, washing machines, dryers, water heaters, freezers—all such white goods have scrap value for the steel that's in them. Until recently, disposing of white goods has not been a problem. Retailers took them back in trade, garbage haulers picked them up without complaint. The disposal routes for white goods were either to the dump or to the steel-shredding industry for recovery. Then recycling hit a snag. Many large electrical appliances manufactured before 1979 contain parts that are insulated with the toxic compound PCB. In the steel-shredding process, the PCB is set free. And when the Environmental Protection Agency reminded scrap dealers of the agency's tough regulations concerning PCB, dealers began rejecting old appliances, thus raising disposal costs. The PCB problem is expected to fade as the number of pre–1979 washers, dryers, freezers, etc., drop.

Best way to get rid of large appliances: If you are buying new, hauling away the old unit should be part of the deal. Otherwise, negotiate to include this service, and be prepared to pay a little. Your garbage hauler is the only alternative.

Special note about refrigerators and freezers: It is against the law in most places to throw out these white goods without first removing the door or any kind of lock that prevents opening the door from inside. This is to avoid creating a deadly trap for kids at play.

APPLIANCES, SMALL

After calling around, we finally got the phone number of a guy—one guy in a city of millions—who allegedly accepts broken but repairable small appliances from good homes. We called. He was out. We left a message. And never heard. So we slipped our inoperative clock radio in with a bag of clothes for the regular charity pickup. They probably threw it in the trash. If you know a better way to handle this disposal problem, please write.

ASBESTOS

Remember when an asbestos hot pad was a standard item beside the stove? For years asbestos was used in ironing-board covers, even in hair dryers. At one time asbestos was considered the perfect construction material —strong, flexible, fireproof, resistant to chemicals, long-lasting. Those same qualities also make asbestos a health hazard. When asbestos becomes powdery, the fibers can be released into the air, inhaled, and swallowed. Once inside the body, asbestos fibers are a constant irritation. They don't break down biologically. They do cause disease.

Although is it mostly out of sight, much asbestos remains in older homes—wrapped around pipes and furnaces, in plaster, in asbestos-vinyl floor tiles, in ceiling tiles, as wall and ceiling insulation. As long as asbestos fibers are enclosed or tightly bonded to another material that prevents them from circulating through the air, there is no cause for concern.

Best way to get rid of asbestos: Call an expert. If you think you have a problem, don't try to solve it yourself. Since the main use of asbestos in homes is for insulation, an insulation contractor can provide advice. Workers who handle asbestos suit up like spacewalkers to protect themselves from the hazardous fibers.

ASHES
Fireplace Ashes

Wood ashes are rich in potassium. Flowers and vegetables need potassium to grow well and to resist disease. The connection is obvious, "But don't overdo it," a horticulturist advises. "Sometimes people get carried away" spreading ashes so heavily that the balance with other nutrients is upset. At our house, some of the fireplace ashes go under the lilac bushes, but that leaves a large quantity for disposal.

Best way to get rid of fireplace ashes: Spread a judicious amount around plants. Throw the rest in the trash—in a bag so they don't contaminate recyclables.

Human Remains

Human ashes, or "cremains," as the funeral directors call it, can be disposed of in many ways other than the familiar encryptment in church or cemetery. Officially speaking, disposition of a human body is considered final at the crematory. What happens to the ashes is up to the survivors. Just keep it "dignified," says one undertaker. Dignity does not include scattering ashes on any body of fresh water, however. That is considered pollution. Ocean disposal is less restrictive. A Boston mortician recalls chartering a fishing vessel to take the survivors and cremains out for a scattering in the Atlantic. Certain military veterans are eligible for a more elaborate sea ceremony. Upon notification from a military Office of Decedent Affairs, the Navy will assign a ship to take a canister of human ashes out to sea and dispatch it to the ocean bottom. The next of kin receive a flag and a report of the exact latitude and longitude where the cremains were tossed over. If that is too dramatic a finale, one's own backyard is a fine place for spreading ashes or burying a canister. Check with local authorities before disposing of cremains on public lands.

BATTERIES
Car Batteries

*C*ar batteries are in a class almost by themselves. They are one of just two kinds of common household objects that waste experts, frankly, don't know how to manage. (The other problem group, or "special recyclable," as it is known euphemistically, is plastics.) "Lead-acid batteries are a problem to collect, process, and dispose of," the EPA said in a 1988 report. "Although many are recycled, a significant number are not. Many battery recyclers are closing their doors, and many retailers and auto shops will not accept used batteries from the consumer."

It should be noted that the EPA is partly responsible for this problem. In its zeal to protect the environment, the federal agency has enacted some very tough rules about who pays for the cleanup if dumped wastes poison underground water supplies. Under the law, even a well-meaning battery recycler who follows all the rules can be found liable for the neglect of some less responsible company farther around the battery-recycling loop. That is why many battery recyclers have quit the business. Others have given up rather than ride the roller-coaster prices of lead. Though the price has risen lately—from 20 cents a pound in 1986 to 40 cents in 1988—it will probably fall again. Commodities prices do that, the experts remind us.

Five years ago at least 90% of old car batteries were recycled nationally. Today the figure is estimated at no higher than 80% and may be as low as 60%. In Minnesota, a very environment-aware state, the Pollution Control Agency believes that 400,000 of the 1 million dead batteries removed from cars each year are dumped in the trash like ordinary, nontoxic wastes, "releasing 7.6 million pounds of lead and 400,000 gallons of sulfuric acid into the environment," according to one report.

Best way to get rid of a car battery: Insist on a trade-in, even if you have to pay a dealer to take it off your hands. Some auto-parts retailers have kept their $5 trade-ins in force despite the punk recycling market. But many service stations have not been so farsighted and flatly refuse old batteries. States are beginning to respond. Minnesota and Florida now require everyone who sells batteries to accept old ones. Suffolk County, New York, has adopted a $5 deposit law. A growing number of states prohibit dumping car batteries in landfills. There are signs of change for the better. But until the recycling loop surrounds all car batteries, it will be up to individual car owners—and let's not forget motorboat, snowmobile, and aircraft owners—to be vigilant.

Dry Cells and Button Batteries

These are the little batteries that power flashlights, radios, clocks, calculators, hearing aids, watches—and toys. As all kids know, Santa Claus maintains a huge warehouse of batteries for toys, most of which wear out around January 10. After that, perpetuating the holiday spirit is up to the generosity of Santa's helpers. Giving shares of battery-company stock would seem a more thoughtful gift than replacing dead batteries, but the kids would never understand.

The big worry about household batteries is mercury—practically all contain small quantities of this toxic metal. Some also contain silver or cadmium. Exposure to mercury can cause mental retardation in humans, and cadmium is linked with cancer. Although the manufacturers say there is no proven risk to throwing worn-out household batteries in the trash, others disagree. Battery-collection programs are popping up around the country. In the Minneapolis area, for example, the first collection campaign was designed to intercept the large number of batteries thrown out immediately after Christmas (40% of all battery sales are made during the Christmas season). In a 23-county area in southwest Missouri, stores that sell hearing aids accept the small batteries for recycling. Some hospitals also accept hearing-aid batteries for recycling. In New York City, where an estimated 8,000 to 10,000 button-cell batteries are thrown in the trash every day, the Environmental Action Coalition has enlisted 185 jewelers and camera stores in a recycling program. The batteries are shipped to a mercury refiner to recover the metal.

Best way to get rid of small household batteries: If possible, route them to a collection program like one of those described above. But there are very few of these nationwide. Your only choice may be to throw old button batteries and dry cells in the trash.

BIRD-CAGE LINERS

The stuff that drops on bird-cage liners is rich in nitrogen and phosphorus and makes good fertilizer for indoor plants. Deep doodoo will nourish an indoor forest. For still another intrahousehold connection, consider lining the cage with confidential papers marked for disposal —old tax returns, love letters, etc. Thus, as the guano deepens, you will not only be protecting the cage but also fouling the papers beyond easy perusal by anyone with spying in mind.

Best way to get rid of bird-cage liners: If you use newspaper, composting is a fine idea. Otherwise send it to the dump or incinerator.

BOOKS

*L*et's say you are moving across town or across country and decide to empty the bookshelves—reduce deadweight, ease back strain. It's time to toss those best-sellers from the sixties. Perhaps you should also pass along Sandburg's four-volume Lincoln set to a deserving youth. And is Sylvia Porter's *New Money Book* for the eighties really worth hauling into the nineties? After careful consideration you have a stack of perfectly good, some mint-condition books to dispose of.

Best way to get rid of books: Contribute them to a neighborhood book sale. Fair weather is the likeliest time for these events, often held outdoors. Libraries and schools raise funds by selling old books at garage-sale prices. Best way to find out when and where is to call your nearest public library.

Most books in home libraries have rummage-sale value at most, a librarian advises. So don't expect any money for them—free pickup is about the best deal you can make. Old textbooks have zero value as books, and old encyclopedias are "dangerous" to pass along, the librarian warns, because they contain outmoded information.

Dipping into an old Colliers or Brittanica is as risky as spooning past-date yogurt, we would guess.

Second best way to get rid of books: Burn them. Hardcover books have practically no value as scrap paper because the bindings clog paper-salvaging machinery. Paperbacks are only marginally interesting to newspaper-collection programs. So let those old plots catch fire one last time: Send them to an incinerator and transform waste into energy. Landfill is the least desirable method of disposal.

With the books dispatched, all that's left for disposal is a golden stack of *National Geographics.* This battalion of old friends has been warping your bookcase for years, and it's time to say good-bye. Good luck! The harsh truth is, no one wants old *Geographics*—least of all libraries, librarians say. Their advice: Give away what you can to kindergarten class for picture cutting. Junk the rest.

BOOZE

We are dealing with opened bottles of beer, wine, and spirits. For some reason you must dispose of the contents. Since transporting opened bottles of booze is illegal in practically all conveyances, including your car, your choices are just about limited to disposal in and around your residence. Shall you pour it down the drain, or place the partially filled containers in the trash?

Best way to get rid of booze: Flush it down the drain with plenty of water, then dispose of the empty container. Compared to empty bottles, partially filled bottles create a greater hazard of flying glass when they are crushed in a garbage packer.

Brake Fluid

Brake fluid contains glycol ethers and heavy metals, hazardous ingredients that should be kept out of landfills.

Best way to get rid of brake fluid: Ask your service station or auto-parts supplier if they'll accept it. Sometimes brake fluid can be recycled with waste oil. If you strike out with dealers, call your state's Environmental Protection Agency for the address of the nearest oil-recycling station. Last option: Save it for the next neighborhood hazardous-waste collection program.

BULLETS

*B*ullets and shotgun shells are considered hazardous waste, no surprise. Mildly surprising is the apparent number of .22, .38, and .45-caliber rounds stashed in households—with the cuff links and pocket change, perhaps, or in a kitchen drawer. The desk sergeant at our local police station says bullets are turned in "with some frequency"—and this is a quiet little town!

Best way to get rid of bullets: Take them to your closest police station. And be prepared to identify yourself—a report will be made.

CARBURETOR CLEANERS

The petroleum distillates in this engine-maintenance chemical will contaminate groundwater supplies if the dump leaks. So don't throw it in the trash.

Best way to get rid of carburetor cleaners: Give to people who work on cars—mechanics, teenagers, and other do-it-yourselfers.

CARS

In the country, a common way to dispose of an old car is to drive it behind the barn, or into the meadow out of sight, and forget the dang thing. There is a certain beauty to this easy method of disposal, considering the headaches abandoned cars cause to city officials. Chicago, for instance, has to haul away about 55,000 derelict cars a year. Moving each one costs roughly $100 for tow truck and driver, and $5 each day it's stored. The city recovers perhaps $40 selling the old hulk to a local scrap-iron dealer—if the dealer is buying. Big if. The car-shredding industry is subject not only to the ups and downs of steel prices but also to state environmental regulations. Massachusetts, for example, shut down all car shredders during part of 1988, out of concern that the shredding process was creating a leftover, called "fluff," that was contaminated with oily hazardous waste. Lacking a local market, New England junk-car dealers had to find buyers in Canada.

Best way to get rid of old cars: Assuming the car has no remaining value as a vehicle, sell it to an auto-wrecking company listed in the Yellow Pages. If there's still some cannibal demand for the car and you don't live too far

away, the wrecker may come pick it up. Otherwise, you'll have to deliver. Prices paid for ordinary old cars reflect their value as scrap metal—generally, $25 to $50. And you have to have title to the car to sell it.

CAR WAX

*C*ar wax and chrome polish contain petroleum distillates, which are hazardous wastes. If you throw them in the garbage can, there's an 80% chance they'll wind up in a landfill, where the toxics can be drawn into underground water supplies.

Best way to get rid of car wax: Give away the unused portion to a car buff. Kids in a high-school auto class should be interested. Otherwise, save it for the neighborhood household hazardous-wastes cleanup day.

CAT LITTER

We favor dogs at our place, so this entry for cat litter —"kitty" litter, if you prefer—is written with a clear sense of superiority. Dogs do it outside, where the stuff belongs, back on old terra firma, at least until someone walks along. As to a cat's preferences, we are told that the frequency of changing litter depends mostly on human fastidiousness—cats have a higher tolerance than their owners do for dirty litter boxes.

To figure Tabby's weekly contribution to the waste load, we begin with a U.S. pet cat population of 55 million (they slightly outnumber dogs, says the American Veterinary Medical Association). If weekly consumption of cat litter is assumed to be 4 pounds, the weekly cat load is 110,000 tons; annually, 5.7 million tons—more than seven times the weight of disposable diapers, as one measure of comparison.

Best way to get rid of cat litter: Before discarding in the trash, consider getting double duty from the litter by using it to absorb other difficult disposables, such as oily cleaning supplies. If you change your own motor oil and have no place to take the dirty stuff (see "Motor Oil"), cat litter will absorb it and help control oil pollution of water supplies near landfills.

CHEMISTRY SETS

*C*hemistry sets are not what they used to be. Back when we were kids, you could mix up some really strong stuff—we remember burning our nostrils on a whiff of chlorine concocted in a test tube and making pretty decent stink bombs out of sulfur. The chemistry sets sold today are tame by comparison. They are liability-proof (". . . grow crystals, watch distillation in action . . . watch metal rise from bottom of glass tube . . .") and contain fairly innocuous disposables. But if you don't know what is in a chemistry set, play it safe with disposal.

Best way to get rid of chemistry sets: Save to turn in during a household hazardous-waste collection program.

Chlorine Bleach

*T*his familiar laundry liquid should be kept out of landfills. It also should be used by itself—never mixed with other cleaners like ammonia, toilet bowl cleaner, or rust remover.

Best way to get rid of chlorine bleach: Use up according to instructions or give away to another launderer. Bleach that cannot be disposed of any other way may be flushed down the drain with lots of water—unless your sewage system is a cesspool. Big shots of antiseptics like bleach will temporarily wipe out the bacteria that power a septic system.

CHRISTMAS TREES

A new tradition is popping up around the nation during the weeks after Christmas: tree-chipping day. Instead of putting trees out for garbage collection, residents are taking their undressed spruces, balsams, and firs to drop-off centers, where the trees are fed through chippers and transformed into mulch—a gift back to the earth. Austin, Texas, is credited with establishing the first large-scale Christmas tree recycling program. The idea has caught on in Portland, Oregon; Lincoln, Nebraska; Seattle, Philadelphia, Chicago, and San Francisco, among other places.

In most communities the last "ho ho" of Christmas has been the garbage crew's old heave-ho of the tree into the collection truck. But with landfill space at a premium, keeping Christmas trees out of the waste stream has acquired a dollar value. Austin figured it saved as much as $20,000 in landfill costs. Chicago kept 10,000 trees out of the dump, conserving an estimated 1,200 cubic yards of landfill space valued at $48,000. In Philadelphia, Christmas tree recycling gained visibility when a local furniture store launched "Rent-A-Tree." For $20, you lease a six- to eight-foot tree. After the holidays you can get $10 back by returning the tree to a chipping station set up on the store

parking lot—and take as much wood-chip mulch as you want. Boulder County, Colorado, has sunk more than 5,000 Christmas trees to the bottom of county lakes. The trees provide shelter for smaller fish and attract the aquatic insects that fish like to eat.

Best way to get rid of Christmas trees: Recycle as mulch. Otherwise, place the tree at the curb for pickup. It's probably better to burn trees in an incinerator than stuff them in a landfill, but you won't have any control over that decision.

CLOTHING

There are many ways to dispose of used clothing that is clean and in good condition. Practically every town and neighborhood has a thrift shop run by a church, hospital, veterans group, or other social-service organization. Many, like the Salvation Army, provide pickup service. Look under "Social Service Organizations" in the Yellow Pages. Larger cities also have retail stores that buy and sell used clothing. Look under "Clothing Bought & Sold." If your only choice is to trash old clothes, okay. But note that garments made of pure wool or pure cotton can be decomposed along with yard waste in a compost pile (using water, air, heat, and periodic turning) and returned to the earth as a soil conditioner.

Best way to get rid of clothing: If nobody else in the family can use it, give it away to a charitable organization. Especially in cold weather there is a desperate need in urban areas for serviceable winter coats. Chicago, for example, conducts an annual "Coat Drive for the Homeless."

COCKROACH TRAPS AND SPRAYS

You've hung out the NO VACANCY sign at Roach Motel. So the little buggers go in the trash—good riddance. Because chemicals used in bug killers sold to the public are not as toxic as they were a decade ago, the risk of contaminating air and water through the waste-disposal process is diminished. Still, there is good reason for caution.

Best way to get rid of cockroach traps and sprays: Follow directions on the label. Spray cans of roach killer should be set aside for delivery to a hazardous-waste collection program.

COFFEE GROUNDS

*A*s every gardener knows, coffee grounds are good for plants. Like sand, they help break up and aerate the soil. No plants to tend? Toss grounds in the trash and teach your housemates to do the same. For, as every plumber knows, coffee grounds plug pipes.

Computer Paper

*A*t one bank we've heard about, there's a special folder on each desk to intercept scrap computer paper, copy-machine paper, and stationery before it hits the wastebasket. The paper is picked up by mail clerks, accumulated, and periodically packed off for sale to a recycler. The proceeds go into the office coffee-and-pastry fund, a dollars-to-doughnuts system that keeps participation rates high. The doughnut yield will be much less in households, of course. But adding your small volume of home-generated office paper to an office recycling program could be the best method of disposal.

Best way to get rid of computer paper: If recycling through the office is not an option, combine computer and other office-grade paper with newspapers for recycling. Or see if a nursery school is interested—the blank back sides of computer printouts make good surfaces for crayon creations.

If none of the above is convenient, just trash the paper in good conscience. If your garbage goes to a waste-to-energy plant—an incinerator—you're helping fuel a fire that's transformed into steam and electricity. If your garbage is buried, the paper presents little if any threat to the underground water supply, though it does occupy expensive landfill space.

CONCRETE see "Construction Debris," p. 43.

CONFIDENTIAL PAPERS

We're talking about old tax returns, canceled and unused checks, paid-off loans, love letters—things like that. What is the risk of these confidential papers becoming recreational reading for workers down the disposal line? In fact, garbage haulers see so much paper during a shift, it becomes a blur. About all that gets plucked out of the hopper is an occasional stuffed animal to decorate the truck. Your secrets are safe with the Sanitation Department.

Snooping by third parties is something else. Depending on what it discloses, your trash may put you at a disadvantage in the hands of someone with malice in mind. Such cases have wound up in court, where judges have not been sympathetic to plaintiffs seeking protection for their trash. When you place it out for pickup by scavengers, you abandon property rights, courts have ruled. But California protects trashers. In the Golden State it is illegal to look in someone else's refuse until it is being tipped in the truck, which just about limits garbage spying to garbage workers.

Best way to get rid of confidential papers: Shred them at the office. Otherwise, take your choice of the following:

1. The Papal Procedure. When cardinals gather to elect a pope, they burn the ballots. This may not work if you don't have a fireplace.
2. The Flush. Paper torn into small pieces will flush down the toilet. Could be tedious if you have lots to get rid of and may raise a plumber's eyebrows if you jam the john.
3. Home Laundry. Dump papers in a large bucket, fill with laundry bleach and water, soak a day. Repeat if necessary until images disappear. Now you have a soggy mass and some understanding of the de-inking process.
4. Self-destruction. Eat your sensitive papers. Spies do it!
5. Chicken Confidential. In a plastic bag, combine confidential papers with leftover chicken. Fish also works. Seal bag and set out to ripen, then discard with trash. The aroma may attract cats but will repel snoops.

See "Bird-Cage Liners," p. 18, for another suggestion.

CONSTRUCTION
DEBRIS

*D*avid Brinkley, in *Washington Goes to War*, tells about a
Georgetown gardener who could not dispose of thirty-
five landscaping bricks. Every time she put them in the trash,
the garbagemen picked them out and left them on the
sidewalk. Her interrogator at the D.C. Department of
Sanitation explained why—and suggested a solution.

"Madam, our trucks are not allowed to haul
away building materials. If they did, when
anybody remodeled a house, they'd find a huge
pile of lumber and pipe and junk, and they're not
equipped to handle it."

"Then how do I get rid of these bricks?"

"Madam, do you work somewhere in town?"

"Yes, at the Agriculture Department."

"How do you get to work?"

"On the bus."

"All right, here's what you do. Each morning
wrap one brick in a newspaper and take it with
you, and when you get off the bus, leave it on the
seat."

Disposing of construction debris requires imagination and patience. A friend of ours who replaced his rotting wooden front porch got rid of the old one by adding a few pieces of wood to the garbage can each week—for many weeks.

Best way to get rid of construction debris: First remove all recyclables. A certain volume of scrap wood has fireplace value. Usable lengths of studs, joists, and beams are hot items with other home remodelers. Corrugated cartons are generally in demand at paper-recycling centers. Scrap aluminum, like old window frames and doors, brings close to the same per-pound price as aluminum beverage cans. Depending on the number of do-it-yourselfers in your neighborhood, you may be able to dispose of whole building parts—window frames, doors, plumbing, and light fixtures —simply by placing them at the street and labeling them "Free to Good Home." A few communities have organized this interhousehold exchange by setting up a free bazaar of used building materials at a central location. Peterborough, New Hampshire, has done it. After everything useful has been pulled out of the pile, you may be stuck with plaster and plasterboard, concrete, and small pieces of wood, glass, plastic, and metal. Inert, porous materials like concrete rubble makes good drainage under planted areas. The rest of the stuff just goes in the trash—bit by bit.

CORRUGATED BOXES

For much of America, disposal first became a household topic when a load of garbage from Islip, New York, went on a Caribbean cruise. Islip and the wandering barge, *Mobro*, became instant international symbols of the disposal crisis—and fresh material for stand-up comics. But town officials in Islip took the kidding in stride, for as it turns out, this Long Island community knows a lot more about good disposal practices than the saga of the *Mobro* might suggest. Corrugated boxes, for example. Islip is one of the few communities nationwide that collects corrugated boxes at curbside along with the more common recyclables such as cans, bottles, and newspapers. Corrugated boxes constitute highly negotiable trash. To business and industry it has something of the star status that aluminum cans enjoy at the retail consumer level. Nationwide, about 45% of corrugated boxes are recycled, mostly from the business community.

Best way to get rid of corrugated boxes: Recycle. If your town does not collect corrugated boxes from households or accept them at a recycling center, you can get them into the recycling stream at any supermarket. (Don't expect to be paid—this is voluntarism!)

Worst way to get rid of corrugated boxes: Bury them in a landfill, where they occupy extremely expensive space. Example: Islip prohibits corrugated boxes in its landfill and requires local businesses to recycle the material. During one year the town figures it kept 20,000 tons of corrugated boxes out of the dump. At a conservative $50 a ton, that's $1 million of space.

DIAPERS, DISPOSABLE

*A*ccording to industry sources, there are 9.2 million baby bottoms to wrap in the United States, and four out of five are wrapped in disposable diapers. So assuming 7.36 million customers and an average five changes a day, the diaper set contributes about 37 million used products to the waste stream daily, or something more than 13 billion a year.

Only a mother knows how far 13 billion dirty diapers will reach laid end to end. To some observers outside the nursery, however, it is too far. The linings of disposable diapers are made of polypropylene, a versatile plastic also found in squeezable ketchup bottles, among other household items. Critics hold up disposable diapers (figuratively speaking) as arch examples of a throwaway society. In reply, the manufacturers say that their products constitute no more than 0.5% of household waste—roughly 800,000 tons a year.

There is no winning such arguments. But how can 7.36 million babies be wrong?

Best way to get rid of disposable diapers: Recycling is difficult and practically nonexistent. Incineration has some

merit. Made of oil, plastic, when burned, releases a great deal of energy and can be put to work a second time—as steam in an electric turbine, for example. But burning also creates dangerous gases, and some people lack confidence that waste-to-energy plants do an effective job of controlling those gases. We don't agree—incineration has a long history of safe use in Europe and Japan. For now, the argument over disposal is largely academic since 90% of disposable diapers are buried in landfills. Best by acclamation.

DIESEL FUEL

The same disposal procedures apply to diesel fuel, used motor oil, light lubricating oil, lamp oil, and kerosene. The objective is to keep them out of landfills, where contamination of groundwater can occur.

Best way to get rid of diesel fuel: Through the used-oil pickup system at your gas station. Next best possibility, though less convenient, is through an oil-recycling station maintained by your state's Highway Department. Check government listings in the phone book, or an environmental organization.

Next best option: Save oil for a community hazardous-waste cleanup day. When all else fails, waste oil can be poured into a container of absorbent material such as sawdust or cat litter and thrown out with the trash. Waste-oil kits are sold at some auto-supply stores.

For more on the oil-disposal problem, see "Motor Oil," p. 83.

DRAIN CLEANING
PRODUCTS

Drain cleaning products contain chemicals that dissolve grease and break through clogged pipes—strong chemicals like sodium or potassium hydroxide, sodium hypochlorite, hydrochloric acid, and petroleum distillates. If you would prefer not to keep these corrosives in the house, try opening clogged drains with a plunger first. Then flush with boiling water. Follow up with a homemade mix of one quarter cup baking soda and two ounces of vinegar. Repeat as necessary.

Best way to get rid of drain cleaning products: Following instructions on the container, use completely. Then double-check to make sure the container is empty—bottles of liquids should be rinsed. Replace lids and caps before discarding. But note that if you are connected to a septic system and have a large amount to dispose of, it may be wiser not to flush the chemical down the drain. The instructions may indicate that the product is safe for septic tanks. If not, put it aside for a household hazardous-wastes collection.

FAST-FOOD CONTAINERS

*F*ast-food restaurants form a tempting high profile along the American landscape—the way road signs tempt sharpshooters. And it's probable that visibility alone has precipitated at least part of the legislative attack on fast-food packaging. Suffolk County, New York; Los Angeles, Palo Alto, and Berkeley, California; and the entire state of Florida have banned the use of the most popular fast-food container, plastic foam. Other communities are considering doing the same. Those familiar Styrofoam hot-drink cups and "clam shell" containers for burgers and salads may become collectibles if the plastics ban spreads.

Critics of plastic-foam containers cite several problems. Los Angeles, for example, decided to act out of concern that a common process used to make plastic foam employs chlorofluorocarbons—CFCs—which migrate upward in the atmosphere and consume the Earth's ozone layer. That speeds the Earth-warming process known as "the greenhouse effect." Suffolk County voted to ban retail food packaging made of polystyrene and polyvinyl chloride to achieve "two main goals," said a county official: "simplifying solid waste management by preventing some non-biodegradable products from coming into our landfills, and sending a clear and unambiguous message to the plastics industry." The message from Suffolk County, New York, is that it's now time to begin an aggressive and comprehensive recycling program for plastics.

Fast-food containers could be taking a bum rap, or proportionally more than they deserve. "We have a garbage information crisis," says William L. Rathje, anthropologist at the University of Arizona, who studies fresh garbage and digs up old landfills for clues to American life-styles. Rathje believes municipal policymakers are being misled by common misconceptions about what's in the garbage can. Quoting Rathje, *Sierra*, the magazine of The Sierra Club, says fast-food containers "have gained notoriety as major contributors to garbage dumps; most estimates put their share of an average landfill's contents at 20 to 30 percent." But Rathje's landfill digs in Tucson, Chicago, and San Francisco find that fast-food containers "make up less than a third of one percent of dump deposits. Street litter and garish advertising make people think about fast-food packaging. . . ."

Best way to get rid of fast-food containers: Since they take up little space in a landfill and may do more harm burned than buried, throw them out and hope they are landfilled. The plastics industry is at work on better solutions.

FIBERGLASS   see "Insulation," p. 72.

FLEA POWDER   see "Insecticides," p. 70.

FLOOR AND FURNITURE POLISH

*P*olishing is such a virtuous activity, it's hard to believe that polish contains household hazardous wastes like diethylene glycol, petroleum distillates, and nitrobenzene. None should ever be disposed of close to groundwater, as in a landfill.

Best way to get rid of floor and furniture polish: If the container is empty, place in trash. If it contains polish, set it aside for collection in a community household-hazardous-wastes roundup. We've read about a nonhazardous, homemade polish: one part lemon juice to two parts olive or vegetable oil. Sounds sensible—leftovers can be poured on the salad.

FLUORESCENT LIGHTS AND FIXTURES

Is there any more delicate trash than a burned-out fluorescent light? We carry the tube as carefully as (we imagine) a stick of dynamite, place it gently in the can, then stand back and throw in something heavy, hoping the tube breaks into harmless smithereens. At the household end of the disposal chain, fluorescent lights are not considered hazardous—officially, at least. Though the tubes do contain small amounts of mercury, the U.S. Environmental Protection Agency has said it's okay to bury them in landfills, though the EPA frowns on large quantities, like hundreds, going into the dump in one load.

The tubes are one matter. The light fixtures are something entirely different. Fluorescent fixtures contain an electrical part called a ballast. In fixtures manufactured before 1978, the ballast very probably is packed with polychlorinated biphenyls—PCBs—an oily, often black substance regarded as an extreme health hazard.

Best way to get rid of fluorescent fixture containing a suspect ballast: Follow this advice, from the booklet

"Hazardous Wastes from Homes," published by Enterprise for Education:

> If a ballast being discarded does not bear a label stating it contains no PCBs, assume it does and deliver to a hazardous-waste collection program. Ballasts sometimes develop leaks. Any liquid dripping from an overhead fluorescent fixture is probably from the ballast and may be PCB. Have an electrician replace the ballast. Using a polyethylene bag over your hand as a glove, clean up the spills with soapy water and paper towels. Holding the used towels and the ballast with the hand inside the bag, turn the bag inside out with your other hand, leaving the towels and ballast inside. Seal the bag. Wash your hands. Deliver the bag to a hazardous-waste collection program.

FOOD WASTE

*C*ompared to the quantities of other things that go in the trash, Americans don't throw away much food. Only about 8% of U.S. household disposables are food products—bread crusts, lettuce leaves, apple cores, half-eaten hot dogs, and the more upscale kitchen discards. Food is a larger proportion of the disposal load in countries like Belgium, the Netherlands, and Italy. But that doesn't mean they waste more food. It means we throw away larger proportions of other things, like paper.

In most households there are two disposal channels for food waste: through the garbage disposal and down the drain, or into the garbage can. Bear with us for a two-paragraph tour of these alternative disposal routes—it's leading to a point.

Food waste that runs through the disposal is flushed into the sanitary sewer system and travels to a sewage treatment plant. When the treatment process ends, what's left is a large volume of water, called effluent, and a large volume of solids, called sludge. The effluent should be clean enough after processing to discharge into a river or lake without threatening public health. The sludge presents a more challenging disposal problem because there's an awful lot of it. Some sludge is burned, some is landfilled. New York City's sludge currently is dumped in the Atlantic Ocean, a discredited practice that the Big Apple has been ordered to quit no later than 1992. But worldwide, most sludge is spread on the land as fertilizer. Sludge is packed with nutrients. It makes things grow and is good for the soil. Properly treated sludge is a manufactured product with enormous value. Probably the best known U.S. sludge product is Milwaukee's Milorganite brand, which generations of gardeners have used to nurture their flowers and veggies. Getting rid of sludge by burning, burying, or ocean dumping is a huge waste.

Now for the other method of household food disposal—and you probably can guess which way this argument is running. Most food waste placed in the garbage can is buried in a landfill. A small amount is burned. As for good end uses, a tiny fraction of food waste is chopped with other organic material, including paper, and converted by the composting process into a soil-like product.

Best way to get rid of food waste: Send it down the drain. People without garbage disposals are excused, and those with archaic plumbing systems should use discretion. And if your sewage disposal system is a septic field, this method is pointless, of course. Before canning all the table scraps, however, don't forget Fido or Rover as a post-consumer consumer. Our dog, Frango, gets three meals a day.

FUNGICIDES   see "Insecticides," p. 70.

FURNITURE

For ultimate disposal of throwaway furniture, burial in a landfill is more desirable than burning in an incinerator. Upholstered furniture—the most common kind you see at curbside—is a composite of cloth, wire, wood, metal, and stuffing of either natural fiber or plastic. Some of the components are safely burnable, some not, but all can be buried with minimal environmental risk and without occupying too much space. The bulldozers that push, crush, and compact wastes are very effective at reducing bulk.

Best way to get rid of furniture: Assuming it has some service life remaining, there are many equally good options. Organizations like the Salvation Army, Goodwill Industries, and Amvets will pick up furniture in good condition for resale in their stores. Garage sales and for-sale ads attract bargain hunters. To contribute your old but usable furniture free to a needy household, try contacting a community church or social-service agency. Or post a notice at a nearby college or university—students have little money for furniture and a constant need.

GASOLINE

*A*ny non-arsonist who has gasoline to dispose of presumably bought it to fuel an engine—a car engine, perhaps. So the first question is: Why is gasoline ever a household disposal problem? Why not pour it in the tank and go for a ride? One service-station owner has shed some light on this mystery. We were talking about motor oil. Did he, as a community service, accept dirty motor oil from do-it-yourself oil changers? Yes, he did, but . . . The *but* is the risk of getting more than just motor oil in performing this voluntary act. Sometimes, he said, the oil is mixed with gasoline. He thinks this is probably last season's lawn mower or snowblower fuel, which can clog small engines when it has stood around too long. Motorboaters and snowmobilers are other sources of throwaway gasoline.

Best way to get rid of gasoline: Turn it over to your local household hazardous-waste collection center. If there isn't one in your community, call the highest local elected official and explain that you have no way to dispose of an extremely hazardous chemical in your house. A response is virtually guaranteed.

GLASS BOTTLES

*C*onsidering how cheap and harmless it is, glass attracts a lot of attention in trash circles. To set the scene, a few facts: Glass represents about 8% of everything thrown out by U.S. households. Plastics, metals, and food wastes each are in approximately the same proportions. Glass is inert. Buried in a landfill it just sits there—forever. Glass is the cheapest packaging material of consumer products. In finished form as a container, glass costs half the price of plastic or paper, and less than one quarter of the price of metal. The flip side is that glass brings very little as scrap, perhaps 2 cents a pound at the recycling center. Compare that to 45 to 50 cents a pound for aluminum cans.

But comparisons are odorous. Aluminum-can recycling is such a huge success (a 50% plus recycling rate nationally, and growing) that the inevitable question is: If aluminum can do it, why not glass? The short answer is that glass can't do it—not yet, anyway—because there is no comparable cash incentive from the glass industry. Local governments have tried to jump-start glass recycling with bottle-deposit laws. The results have been mixed.

According to one study, New York State's bottle-deposit law

caused glass containers to lose 35% of market share. Who picked it up? Ironically, it was the plastic-bottle manufacturers, whose product is a lot harder to recycle than glass. If they have a choice, grocers will avoid the hassle of sorting and storing deposit bottles by shifting to plastic. California also has a deposit law—a very complicated system that costs $100 million a year—that has increased both recycling rates and opportunities for fraud. Deposit laws also have driven voluntary buyback centers out of business by drawing away the two big attractions: aluminum and glass containers.

It's going to take a while for glass to find its niche. Meanwhile there is exciting news from Vienna, that hotbed of nineteenth-century style. Throughout the Austrian capital, milk is being sold in glass bottles, replacing waxed cartons. The containers are designed to be returned to the dairy, washed, sterilized, and refilled. What a revolutionary idea!

Best way to get rid of a glass bottle: Recycle if convenient —more and more communities provide curbside pickup. Otherwise, trash it. Buried glass does not pollute groundwater.

GLUE

Water-soluble glue, such as white paste and mucilage, can be thrown in the trash without concern. But glue and cement containing solvents other than water—trichloroethane, toluene, and other petroleum distillates, for example—require special handling.

Best way to get rid of non-water-soluble glue: Assuming you can't give it away to someone who uses the stuff, open the glue outdoors in a sheltered place out of reach of children and animals. Let it dry thoroughly. Then throw it away.

See "Rubber Cement," p. 110.

GRASS

Grass clippings form the largest portion of what is called "yard waste," which includes all the greenery, twigs, branches, leaves, flowers past their prime, etc., that we cut, pull, snip, rake, and blow out of garden and lawn. Altogether, this stuff amounts to 18% of household wastes nationwide but up to 40% during some times of the year in some communities—fall in the Frost Belt and all year round in Palm Beach, for example. The U.S. Environmental Protection Agency calculates that we produce 23.8 million tons of yard waste a year, 70% of it grass. (Pound for pound we harvest as much grass from our lawns as Japan harvests rice from all its fields in a year. They sell the rice, we bury the grass.) Yard waste is second only to paper as the largest ingredient of landfills, explaining why there is so much interest in keeping yard waste out of the dump. A handful of states, beginning with New Jersey and Pennsylvania, already have banned yard waste from landfills, and more are expected to follow.

Best way to get rid of grass: Cut it high and let it lie. In a few days the cut grass will wither, fall between the green blades, and fade from view, while you congratulate yourself for practicing the highest and best form of waste disposal, namely creating no waste at all. "Source reduction" is the technical name. Students of this disposal method point out that decaying grass is a natural fertilizer; keeps the soil cooler and wetter, a hedge against dry spells; and forms a pleasant cushion underfoot. The let-it-lie method works best if the grass is kept fairly high—at least three inches—and cut often enough that the clippings are short in proportion to the length of the grass. Lawn experts advise cutting not more than one third the height of grass at one time.

The Bronx cheer you just heard is the other point of view being expressed. Tens of millions of people get a big kick out of transforming an unkempt yard into a buzz-cut picture of orderliness, with the cutting path at neat right angles to the street, or at a daring diagonal. The sense of order is euphoric to the operator. We have known these grassy highs. To the cut-and-bag-it crew, leaving grass clippings on the lawn is worse than leaving your bed unmade.

Motivated by the shortage of landfill space, some communities are beginning to think of yard waste as a cash crop. It's a simple idea: Pick up yard waste separately from other trash, truck it to a large central composting pile, give it air and water, stir occasionally, and before long you have reduced the volume to a fraction of the original and produced what bureaucrats call a "soil amendment." The plain old name is humus—rich in nutrients, good for the earth, and sold by the bag in garden stores everywhere.

Some towns want yard waste piled loosely at the curb for pickup by a vacuum truck or front-end loader; others simply want it in separate containers. There's a new bag on the market made of plastic blended with a small percentage of cornstarch. It's supposed to decompose rapidly, as bacteria feast on the starch. If the idea works, bagged grass and other yard waste will not have to be removed from the container for composting, saving much labor. But whether these bags hold up long enough at the curb and break down fast enough in the compost pile remains to be seen. Another open question is what happens to the plastic residue after bacteria devour the starch. Is it going to sneak into the food chain as a "soil amendment"? And will that become a problem?

King-size grocery sacks also have been used experimentally for leaves and grass, with good results. Given the right amount of moisture and air in a compost pile of proper size, the bags are completely consumed in less than a growing season. But these kraft-paper bags cost three times more than plastic, don't hold as much, and are hard to close.

Worst way to get rid of grass: Landfill it. Contrary to popular belief, landfills are not simply large compost piles. Comparatively little decomposition occurs in a dump—seldom more than 20% by volume. We can do much better than that—80% plus—in an aboveground compost pile.

GREASE

*G*arage and machine-shop grease should be disposed of like oil (see "Motor Oil," p. 83). We're talking here about animal fat: goose grease, bacon grease, chicken fat, etc. Animal fat may clog kitchen pipes, but it presents no other special disposal problem, either in sewage-treatment plant, incinerator, or landfill. The main idea is to prevent cooking grease from soaking into other household disposables that could be pulled from the waste stream and recycled if clean, such as paper and cardboard.

Best way to get rid of grease: Collect in a can kept in the refrigerator, then dispose of congealed grease in the trash.

INSECTICIDES

This little sermon applies to fungicides, pesticides, and insecticides. Among all the chemicals used around the home, this threesome is the most treacherous. One big problem, say people who worry about it professionally, is the lack of an adequate warning printed on the product of the possible long-term health risk to humans from coming in contact with the "-cides." The warning on a pack of cigarettes is a lot stronger and clearer. Another big problem is inadequate instruction to the user about proper disposal.

Here are two simple rules concerning the use and disposal of fungicides, pesticides, and insecticides. One, use them as if they cause cancer. Two, never throw unused quantities or empty containers in the trash—the risk of residues getting into water supplies through landfills is simply too great. Let's add a third rule: Read and follow directions on the label, but let Rules One and Two prevail.

Best way to get rid of insecticides, fungicides, and pesticides: The best method of disposal begins with purchase. Since your objective is to have none to get rid of, calculate your needs very carefully and then ratchet down a notch or two. Underestimate. It's better to run out following normal application than to run over. If you're stuck with quantities of these chemicals, the first prudent disposal procedure is to give them away to another user. A neighbor may have a need. A commercial nursery or garden shop may accept small leftover quantities in the original container. Your second and last option for disposal is to set the products aside for collection in a community household-hazardous-waste program. Your local government will know when and where. In rural areas, the county agricultural office should have information. End of sermon.

INSULATION

*P*eople know insulation as the pink fiberglass fluff
stuffed inside walls and above ceilings, or as a yellow
or pink wrap for pipes. Mineral-wool and cellulose
insulation are blown loose into wall cavities and attic floors.
New construction may be insulated with sheets of
expanded plastic. If you have insulation on your hands,
presumably it is left over from a construction project.

Best way to get rid of insulation: Don't get rid of it—apply
it. If you have access to an unheated attic, basement, or
crawlspace, you'll probably see opportunities to tack up,
spread out, or stuff in the leftovers, even if you simply add
to what is already in place. Remember that insulation
blocks sound as well as heat. If no further applications are
apparent, store the insulation for possible future use, or
give it away. But don't throw it out. Insulation is long-
lasting, nonpolluting, and beneficial—a rare combination
these days.

JUNK MAIL

"**O**h, God, we get thousands!" said the lady at the Direct Mail Marketing Association. "In a slow week, maybe 3,000 letters; and calls all the time." We were talking about requests from addressees who want their names removed from mailing lists. Yes, you really can do that, by calling or writing the DMMA (212-689-4977, 6 East 43 St., New York, New York 10017). Your name and address will be added to the next quarterly edition of the do-not-mail list circulated to 20,000 or so mail-order companies—"mostly catalog companies but some sweepstakes and charitable," the lady said. "You'll see less mail coming in after a few months," she promised.

And none too soon. We did a count of the mail that arrived at our house last October 31. Out of thirty-three pieces of mail stuffed in our box, we tallied one party invitation; two bills, one piece of personal correspondence containing a photocopy inscribed, "Thought you'd like to see"; three each of newsletters and magazines; and twenty-three pieces of junk mail. The volume just keeps growing. Our mailman is looking more and more like the Sorcerer's Apprentice.

Let's make one thing clear: We do read or at least scan our

junk mail, and we don't believe people who say they don't. Receiving a large volume of advertising confirms our positions as card-carrying members of the Consumer Society. When we complain about getting duplicate copies of the Sharper Image catalog, we are actually making a statement about our life-style. We only wish *National Geographic* would quit nominating us for membership.

Best way to get rid of junk mail: Stop it at the source by notifying the Direct Mail Marketing Association, as described above. (To stop pornographic mail from coming to your house, fill out Form 2201 at your post office.)

KEROSENE see "Diesel Fuel," p. 50.

LAMP OIL see "Diesel Fuel," p. 50.

LEATHER GOODS see "Clothing," p. 36.

LEAVES

We caught a whiff of burning leaves one weekend last fall. The fire might have been illegal, but it sure smelled good. How long has it been since leaf burning was declared un-American? Thirty years? Air pollution was the big concern, and leaves were a big, visible target. Now leaves are in trouble again. They occupy too much space in landfills. Leaves and other "yard waste" such as grass, flowers, twigs, weeds, etc., compose about 18% of household trash annually. During fall in the North, the proportion can jump to 40%. We know the exact weekend when leaf production peaked at our place—it was a beautiful, late November day, and we must have hauled thirty plastic sacks of leaves to the curb. Leaf raking is an annual rite. We prefer to let them all drop, then make one clean sweep before the snow flies. It's good for household morale but a dirty trick on garbage haulers.

Because leaves are such a large part of the waste load and have commercial value as compost, many communities have banned leaves from landfills or soon are planning to. This conserves landfill space and buys time to find better disposal options for all wastes. In New Jersey, Pennsylvania, New York, and Massachusetts, composting is fast becoming the major leaf-disposal method. Wellesley, Massachusetts, is credited with establishing one of the first municipal leaf composting programs. In a recent collection season, 1400 tons of leaves—the equivalent of about 60 garbage-truck loads—were dumped at the Wellesley composting center. The mulch created by decomposition is used on city land, or traded for trees at local nurseries. In Burlington, Vermont, the city has worked a deal with a garden-supply store to serve as a leaf drop-off center. Add your leaves to the pile and you get a coupon worth one bushel of compost next season.

But let's face it, most people with leaves to get rid of would prefer a rapid, curbside solution to their problem. The big question is what to put the leaves in. Traditional plastic bagging is okay if the leaves are still going to a landfill, but when your community begins composting, some other procedure will be required: perhaps just dumping leaves loose at the curb. (Also see "Grass," p. 66.)

Best way to get rid of leaves: We don't practice this method but feel duty bound to advocate it—composting at home. The process is not as dirty, smelly, or labor-intensive as many people believe. A compost pile can be as casual as a mound of leaves, grass, withered flowers, and vegetable tops located in some obscure corner of the property. The pile requires only air, water, occasional stirring, and time. Give it what it needs and success is virtually guaranteed. You can hasten the process by stirring in small amounts of dirt and leftover fertilizer. Chewing up the leaves with a lawn mower before dumping will speed things along, too.

LYE   see "Oven Cleaners," p. 92.

Magazines

*L*arge quantities of discarded magazines used to wind up over people's heads—as fiber in roofing paper. Then fiberglass came along and took much of that market away. And then magazines began using a tough glue binding that holds pages tight but does not recycle gracefully in paper-recycling mills. So, while other members of the paper family command respect from the secondary market, magazines frequently are considered contaminants. The glue binding remains a barrier, and the paper is coated with materials that turn to sludge in the pulping process. Nevertheless, some magazines find their way into low-end uses like chipboard and boxboard, or are shipped to mills overseas.

Best way to get rid of magazines: We're tempted to leave them in our internist's waiting room, where old magazines never die. But the practical solution for now is to toss them in the trash for burning or landfilling.

MATTRESSES   see "Furniture," p. 61.

MEDICINES

*B*est way to get rid of expired prescriptions and other medicines: Flush down the toilet, rinse the container, and discard. This avoids exposing innocent but curious people, like kids, to the possible hazards of playing with medicine fished from the trash.

Best way to get rid of a hypodermic syringe: Break off the needle at the hub, place both syringe and needle in an empty plastic bottle—a bleach or soft drink bottle, for example. Screw the cap on the bottle and discard in trash. This procedure will render the syringe useless and protect trash handlers from accidental injury during disposal.

MIRRORS AND MISCELLANEOUS GLASS

Glass containers like soda bottles and food jars are recyclable. But mirrors, glass cookware, lead-based glass such as crystal, TV tubes, window glass, and light bulbs are made of additional materials that do not fall neatly into the glass recyclers' melting pots. The marketplaces for these glass items, such as fiberglass mills, terrazzo factories, and asphalt paving plants, are hard to find.

Best way to get rid of all of the above: If usable, give to a charitable organization that collects household items. If not usable, throw in the trash.

MOTHBALLS

Who buys mothballs? Someone must; we've seen them for sale. But the last time we recall using any was a long time ago—to keep bugs out of the garden. We haven't seen a moth in decades and suspect that they have been done in by air-conditioning, polyester, and one-hour dry cleaning. Mothballs contain naphthalene, which is derived from coal tar or petroleum. Mothballs or flakes thrown in the garbage will probably be buried in a landfill, where the naphthalene can be leached into the groundwater, polluting it.

Best way to get rid of mothballs: Don't throw them in the trash—use up completely. If you can't stand the smell within living quarters, consider placing them to evaporate (out of a child's reach) in some other place that should be kept pest-free, such as an attic or basement.

MOTOR OIL

A physician we know buys motor oil by the case and makes the periodic change of lubricant himself on his Porsche and his wife's Dodge. He disposes of the motor oil in the car-care bays of a nearby full-service department store. Whether he also buys his oil there, he does not say, not wishing to violate a professional confidence, we imagine.

More people change their own motor oil than you might guess. The U.S. Environmental Protection Agency reports that do-it-yourself oil changers generate 350 million gallons of used oil a year. Assuming two cars, five quarts per change, and four changes a year (if you do it yourself, you do it often!), there could be as many as 17 million people out there who apparently enjoy crawling under the engine, wrenching open a greasy plug, and catching and disposing of dirty lubricant.

A study of do-it-yourself oil changers in Minnesota reveals that they are, except for this curious behavior, very much like other people. Typically they maintain two cars and put about 12,000 miles a year on each. The majority live in metropolitan areas, and the majority also disposes of used oil in an environmentally acceptable manner.

But the majority who do not so dispose of motor oil have the means to wreak havoc on nature, and probably already have. Some oil changers pour the old stuff on roads for "dust control." Some pour it on the ground without any reason, or down a storm sewer. Some slip it in the trash, a nice surprise for sanitation workers as jugs of oil, compressed by the garbage packer, pop open and spray truck, garbage, and workers with hydrocarbons plus various additives, none benign.

That's the problem with dumping of motor oil; it finds its way back to you, usually as it infiltrates and contaminates water supplies. Motor oil never wears out or breaks down in the environment. It gets dirty in use, but once the dirt is removed, it can be used again with the same effectiveness as the virgin product.

Recycling rates are sensitive mostly to the price of virgin oil. Back when OPEC had a hammerlock on the market and crude was $30 plus a barrel, dirty motor oil brought up to 30 cents a gallon. Recycling was convenient at neighborhood service stations because the owner was making a little money as middleman. But when OPEC collapsed, it dragged the value of used oil down, too—to zero. If a service-station owner knows he will receive even one cent per gallon for used oil, he'll cooperate. But at zero cents, recycling needs an official push.

A few states and communities are trying to make it easy for do-it-yourself motor-oil changers to dispose of the old stuff the right way. For example, on garbage day in Milpitas, California, residents place used motor oil at the curb in old milk or bleach bottles. The garbage collectors pour the oil into a small holding tank fitted to the truck especially for this purpose. It's drained at the garage into a larger recycling tank. Alabama has a statewide system of oil-collection centers called Project Rose. Alexandria, Virginia, uses utility-bill inserts to remind residents about the location of ten local service stations that accept used oil under the state oil-recycling program (which raises a human-relations matter; as one do-it-yourselfer told the Minnesota survey, he would be embarrassed to walk into any service station with dirty oil he had changed himself).

Best way to get rid of motor oil: If a recycling opportunity like one of those described above is not available in your community, save the oil for delivery to a household hazardous-waste collection. If that isn't a possibility, either —and as a last resort—pour the oil into a plastic bag filled with an absorbent material like cat litter and dispose of it in the trash.

NAIL POLISH AND REMOVER

*B*est way to get rid of nail polish: Remove the cap and let the container stand open for a few days. The polish will solidify, rendering it harmless in a landfill. Toss.

Best way to get rid of nail-polish remover: Flush contents down the toilet, rinse the container, and toss it.

NEWSPAPERS

Your trash can contains more paper than anything else. In its many varieties, paper averages 41% of what is called the "municipal solid-waste stream." To prove this number, try fishing all the paper out of your own solid-waste stream and see how much new disposal space you have created. Newspapers, mail, magazines, butter cartons, tissue boxes, butcher paper, deli wrappings, pizza cartons . . . On second thought, assign this project to a resident Cub Scout for extra credit. You'll keep your hands clean, and he'll learn something. Paper provides a number of elementary lessons in the economics of trash.

Consider newspaper, the most common kind of paper found in household trash. Let's say the cost to dump newspaper (or anything else) in a crowded East Coast landfill is $100 a ton. Steep price—but wait! There's an option: Instead of dumping the stuff, you can sell it to a recycler for $50 a ton. Easy choice—you trundle your bundles of news to the recycler, pocket $50, and save $100 in "avoided" costs: a landfill interment that never happened.

Now, let's say the recycler's warehouse is chock full of old news. He doesn't need to buy any more for a while, so he lowers his offering price to zero. He'll take the stuff off

your hands, but he won't pay you. Still a good deal? Of course it is, because you are still avoiding the certain $100 cost of your only alternative.

Now, let's say the supply of old news takes a terrific jump because the new citywide, curbside recycling programs are a huge success. So much newspaper is stacking up at the recycler's plant that disposal is becoming a problem for him. He quits accepting paper free and starts charging you $50 a ton. Still a good deal? Clearly not as good a deal as before, and you may begin to wonder where disposal costs are headed.

Recently, certain Eastern cities were wondering exactly that, as the newspaper lesson we sketched above began to be played out in real life. The extreme landfill shortage in the East, parts of the West Coast, and certain Midwestern pockets has driven disposal costs to record levels. Seeking relief, cities have cranked up new programs to intercept trash on its way to the dump, divert it to recycling markets, and avoid at least part of the high cost of dumping.

Household newspaper recycling is an old idea that predates even the recycling of aluminum cans. For the most part, it has been a suburban phenomenon, teaching lessons in conservation and voluntary fund-raising to generations of kids. But now the lessons are being applied on a mandatory, massive scale in major cities. As huge new quantities of old newspaper surge into the recycling market, small-scale volunteer programs have become an endangered species.

But trade-offs are common as new industries develop. While the volunteer programs fade away, new jobs are created in newspaper collection and recycling. And as the volume of recycled paper grows, old jobs in the pulpwood industry disappear.

About one third of the newsprint made in the United States is made from recycled newspaper. Sounds impressive until you add that two thirds of U.S. newsprint consumption is paper manufactured in Canada from virgin pulpwood. If recycling saves trees, two out of three are north of the border! Let's take this further: The single largest export from the Port of New York is wastepaper, and the U.S. is the major exporter of wastepaper in the world. The major importers include Taiwan, Mexico, South Korea, and Japan. Tracing the global possibilities, a piece of newsprint made from pulpwood in Ontario could become a newspaper in Ohio, then a clock-radio carton in Osaka, and finally a facial tissue in Oskaloosa. And you thought newspaper recycling was boring!

Best way to get rid of newspapers: Bundle it for separate

collection. And don't be discouraged if you hear that some newspaper intended for recycling winds up in a landfill or incinerator. The supply of old news is expected to run generally ahead of demand for five or six years more years, until new processing plants are on-line.

OVEN CLEANERS

The active ingredient is sodium hydroxide (lye), also found in drain openers. Presumably, the quantity to be disposed of is a smallish leftover not worth giving away —as a hostess gift, for example.

Best way to get rid of oven cleaners: Flush down the toilet. Rinse the empty container, taking care not to splash on hands or face. Throw container in the trash.

PAINT

William L. Rathje, the University of Arizona anthropologist who studies garbage for insights into American culture, says you can tell what kind of neighborhood you're in by looking only in the garbage cans. He finds especially reliable clues among the disposables classified as household hazardous wastes. Rathje says that in a poor neighborhood you see lots of motor oil, brake fluid, carburetor cleaner, engine de-gunker, car-body repair debris, and other leftovers from do-it-yourself auto maintenance. In a wealthy neighborhood you find herbicides, pesticides, and other gardening chemicals. But in a middle-class neighborhood you find every color of the American Dream—in a home handyman's larder of paint and painting supplies. Latex paint, oil paint, paint stripper, varnish remover, metal primer, wood primer, gummy paint rollers, paint brushes stiff with rigor mortis.

People who paint their dwellings wind up with leftovers. We think this has less to do with paint selling than the do-it-yourselfer's anxiety about running out of supplies after the store closes but before the project is done. Maybe the explanation is that paint comes in gallon cans. Whatever the reason, home painters who are not corporate Gypsies seem prone to accumulate shelves of partly filled paint

cans. They are kept for a rational reason, to touch up the old paint job. But if our experience is typical, we suspect that the majority of leftover paint cans are never opened again.

Tossing paint in the trash creates two potential hazards. There's a risk of injury to the garbage collectors if a paint can pops and spews its contents as it is being compacted in the truck. But the long-term problem is contamination of drinking water as paint leaks into the landfill and finds its way into the underground water supply.

Best way to get rid of all paint: Take it to a free paint exchange. The idea is, local residents bring paint to the community paint swap shelf and help themselves to new hues. The city of Santa Monica, California, collected 2,500 gallons of paint in the first fifteen months of a paint exchange and recirculated more than 600 gallons to residents. (The city also converted a large portion of the oil paint into fuel for a cement kiln, and extra latex paint was reprocessed as graffiti cover.)

Best way to get rid of latex paint: Dry and toss. If you can't give the stuff away, open the lid and let it dry out. This process can be hastened with the addition of sand or cat litter. When the paint has solidified, it's okay to toss in the trash. Water-based latex paint is usually not considered a hazardous waste after it has dried solid.

Best way to get rid of oil-based paint: Treat as a hazardous waste. Oil-based paint contains many hazardous chemicals, including metals and solvents. It's very important to keep these things out of landfills. In many communities, residents are periodically invited to bring all their leftover hazardous wastes to a central collection point for safe disposal. Oil paint usually makes up a large part of the roundup. If that's not an option for you, experts advise following the same procedure as for latex paint—opening the paint can in a well-ventilated place, letting it dry until the contents are solidified, then tossing it in the trash.

PAINT BRUSH CLEANER AND THINNER

*P*aint thinners such as mineral spirits and turpentine often are used in place of specifically formulated brush cleaners. Disposal procedures are the same. And judging from our own lazy behavior, we suspect that many gallons of these toxic products are thrown out before their time. At the end of a project with oil-based paint, we just want to get the stuff off our hands and admire our handiwork. Not so fast, profligate!

Best way to get rid of paint thinner—mineral spirits and turpentine: Recycle on home projects. This requires two plastic jugs, like milk or juice bottles; coffee filters; and a funnel. Pour soiled thinner into a clean jug. Set aside until most of the solids settle. Then decant through filter (in funnel) into the second clean jug. What you have left is sludge in the first bottle and reusable paint thinner in the second. The sludge bottle should be kept for disposal during a community roundup of household hazardous wastes. It may also be combined with oil-based paint being held for disposal.

Best way to get rid of paint brush cleaner: Follow the same procedure as above.

PAINT STRIPPER

If you are unable to give away leftovers and insist on disposing of this strong stuff, first read the contents label to see if the stripper contains lye (sodium hydroxide) or methylene chloride.

Best way to get rid of stripper containing lye: Taking care not to splash on your hands or face, flush it down the drain with lots of water. Rinse the container and discard.

Best way to get rid of stripper containing methylene chloride: Take to a household hazardous-waste collection program. If that's not an option, think again about giving it to someone—a janitor? a furniture refinishing shop?

PAPER BAGS

To give newspaper recycling a kickoff in San Francisco, the two daily newspapers stuffed a "starter kit"—a paper grocery bag—into each copy delivered one day. Instructions printed on the bag said to use it as a container for a week's worth of newspapers and then recycle. Which reminds us that paper bags have so many good second uses, it ought to be a felony to throw them away empty.

Best way to get rid of paper bags: Fill with some other disposable. Since paper is biodegradable, it's the ideal container for other biodegradables, such as garbage and yard waste. In some households, miscellaneous small paper bags go to school and work as lunch bags. Paper bags from the grocery store are cousins of corrugated cardboard boxes and are properly added to this kind of paper for recycling.

PESTICIDES   see "Insecticides," p. 70.

PETS, DECEASED

The American Veterinary Medical Association estimates the number of cats, dogs, birds, and horses kept by Americans at 126 million. With other creatures added in—fish, snakes, rabbits, hamsters, etc.—the total rises to more than 200 million, approaching parity with the human population. In many households, pets do enjoy parity as family members, making human decisions difficult when a pet dies.

Best way to get rid of a deceased pet: Do what feels best, and there are numerous possibilities. Except for very large animals, burial on your property is an option. City ordinances typically require burial of domestic animals at least three feet below the surface. Many animal shelters will accept deceased pets for cremation with other animals at no charge, though a donation will be welcomed. Depending on pet and owner, disposal in the garbage can may be the best way, but check with the garbage hauler first. Many communities also have a pet cemetery. The Yellow Pages in our community lists several, including one that provides pickup service, grief counseling, individual cremation, formal burial, caskets, memorials, and cremation urns. In some communities, vets can arrange to have a pet's body sent to a rendering plant for disposal. Rendering transforms the carcass into useful products such as soap and fertilizer, and that could have appeal if recycling is important to the owner.

PIPE

"*A* piece of old Yankee advice," an old colleague said on apt occasions. "Never throw away a piece of metal." We've kept the faith, moving a growing collection of metal from house to house. And we've never lacked the odd screw, bolt, nail, spring, angle iron, flat plate, or piece of pipe. Save it all—you never know when you'll need it. Just a piece of old Yankee advice.

PLASTER   see "Construction Debris," p. 43.

Plastic Bags

*B*acteria, they say, love the idea: edible garbage bags. You bury the bag in a landfill, and *chomp, chomp, chomp*, the landfill bugs burp with pleasure. The scientific name for this process is biodegradability. A small amount of cornstarch is blended with the plastic. The bacteria nibble on the cornstarch and the plastic falls to pieces. Where the plastic actually goes, no one quite knows, and that does raise some eyebrows.

But the more important question is how much biodegrading actually occurs in a landfill. In fact, much less than is commonly believed. Excavations of old dump sites have unearthed 30-year-old garbage more or less intact. Over decades there may be as much as a 20% reduction in the volume of buried garbage—very little compared to the 80% reduction in a backyard compost pile. The difference? A general lack of air and water under ground.

The other product out of the plastics lab that has people excited (mostly people who make plastic bags) is the photodegradable bag, made of plastic that turns brittle and breaks up in sunlight. This has been proposed as the easier way to get rid of plastic litter—easier than modifying human behavior, for example. Photodegrading does require patience—several months of sunlight. If the process works anywhere, it ought to work in Florida. And right on cue, the Florida legislature has proposed that businesses using plastic carryout bags must use bags made of material that degrades within 120 days. Long enough to get home from the store, anyway.

Best way to get rid of plastic bags: There is no best way at the moment. Only 1% of plastic disposables presently are being recycled. Everything else is buried or burned. But hopeful news comes out of Vermont, where one trash entrepreneur has found a buyer for large quantities of polyethylene bags, such as dry-cleaning and vegetable-produce bags. They command up to 30 cents a pound, second only to aluminum in scrap value. For your conversion chart, there are twelve dry-cleaning bags to a pound, or about the same as aluminum cans.

PLASTIC BOTTLES

Aluminum is aluminum and glass is glass. But plastic is a variety of incompatible chemicals, explaining in part why so little plastic is being pulled out of the trash for second uses, and why so much is being buried or burned. In a recent year, 75,000 tons of plastic soda bottles were recycled. But compare: 616,000 tons of aluminum cans to 1.5 million tons of glass. Plastic bottles lack a success model. The melting and re-forming process does not sterilize plastic as it does aluminum and glass. For that reason, recycled plastic cannot be returned to the marketplace as a container of food or drink.

Many other useful things can be made of used plastic, however. Bathtubs, car bumpers, lumber, strapping, storage bins, carpets, moldings, sewer pipes—there are dozens of good uses for various plastics. The challenge is to sort plastic trash into its categories. The plastics industry has started helping this process along by identifying what containers are made of with a number molded on the bottom. For example: 1 for soda bottles made of PET, polyethylene terephthalate; and 2 for milk and laundry jugs of HDPE, high-density polyethylene.

Progress in plastic-bottle recycling cannot come fast enough to satisfy the critics. There is something about the whole topic of plastic trash that causes people to lose their tempers. It could be the weight/volume matter. Though plastics of all kinds constitute just 7% of all household waste by weight—a little less than glass—they form almost 25% by volume. They are bulky and hard to compress. Despite all these physical things, however, plastic has always had an image problem: It's cheap, and cheap is inferior.

Just the same, if you feel guilty throwing plastic bottles in the trash when you know other people are recycling them, you may be ripe for reform. Designers of recycling programs have found that adding plastic bottles to collection programs is very effective at increasing overall participation.

Best way to get rid of plastic bottles: Take a guilt trip— return them for deposit if there's a redemption program in your area. Second best, separate them from other trash for recycling.

RAT AND MOUSE POISON

Rodents sometimes can be controlled using old-fashioned, baited traps. Doing so avoids the complications of proper disposal of unused poisons.

Best way to get rid of rat and mouse poison: Follow the directions on the label concerning disposal. But also read "Insecticides," p. 70. The same precautions apply.

RUBBER CEMENT

*B*est way to get rid of rubber cement: Unscrew cap and let contents solidify. Then throw it in the trash. Although the liquid cement contains chemicals that will pollute groundwater, the risk of harmful substances leaking out in a landfill is greatly reduced by letting the cement harden. Around our house, turning the glue pot hard is no special problem—it always seems to be that way.

Rugs

What you see piled at the street usually is wall-to-wall carpeting made of synthetic fibers. Presumably it has lost all value as a floor covering.

Best way to get rid of rugs: Roll or fold as neatly as possible and place out with a FREE sign. It is better to get these bulky items into some kind of secondary use, such as padding for a horse stall, than to dump or burn them.

RUST REMOVER

We once bought a pint of rust remover called "Naval Jelly." It's still on the shelf some years later, unopened. You never know when rust will strike. But if we ever have to dispose of our "Naval Jelly," we'll know what to do.

Best way to get rid of rust remover: Flush down the toilet. Rinse the container before discarding.

Septic Tank Cleaners

Septic tank and cesspool degreasers that contain organic solvents—petroleum distillates, for example—may dissolve grease, but they also pass through the septic system and into the earth, posing a threat to groundwater. Experts advise against using such cleaners and adopting a preventive strategy: diverting food fat into a container for disposal in the trash.

Best way to get rid of septic tank cleaners containing organic solvents: Put aside for the next household hazardous-waste collection.

SHOE POLISH

*B*est way to get rid of shoe polish and dye: Open the container and let the contents dry thoroughly. Then throw in the trash.

SHOES see "Clothing," p. 36.

Six-Pack Yokes

The plastic punch-out that connects soft drinks and beer cans is a brilliant packaging innovation—cheap, strong, sleek, easy to hold. Unfortunately it's also long-lasting. If Jacques Cartier & Co. had popped a six-pack on the banks of the St. Lawrence in the year 1534 and left the trash behind, the plastic connector would remain more or less intact today. Plastic persists, as we are reminded by six-pack yokes strewn by the roadside and floating in lakes and seas. The litter factor has prompted at least two states, Minnesota and Florida, to take legal aim at six-pack yokes with proposals to ban them entirely. There is some interest in new, degradable plastics—one breaks down in sunlight, the other when attacked by bacteria—as an answer to plastic litter. But such a solution would seem to run at cross-purposes with simultaneous efforts by the plastics industry to make recycling of all plastics easier.

Best way to get rid of six-pack yokes: At the moment few people have a choice but to trash them. When plastics recycling becomes more widely available, there will be better options.

SMOKE DETECTORS

Molded inside the plastic cover of one of our smoke detectors are these words: "CAUTION—Contains radioactive material . . . return for repair or disposal." If your smoke detector is the ionization type, it contains the same warning. If you cannot tell, assume that it does. If you are disposing of the smoke detector because it has been accidentally damaged, handle it like a hazardous waste: Pick it up with your hand in a plastic bag, then turn the bag inside out around the smoke detector, and seal the bag.

Best way to get rid of smoke detectors: Don't throw it in the trash and don't take it to a hazardous-waste collection —radioactive materials are not accepted. Return it to the manufacturer or retailer.

SPRAY CANS

If there's any pressure left in a spray can, it can explode during rough handling in the garbage collection or disposal process. That creates a possible hazard to workers. The other problem is what's inside the can—many contain chemicals that should be kept away from drinking water supplies (see "Paint," p. 93).

Best way to get rid of spray cans: If the can is empty and contains no pressure, toss it in the garbage. If the spray tip is clogged and you cannot relieve any residual pressure or evacuate the contents, set it aside for delivery to your neighborhood hazardous-waste center.

STEEL (TIN) CANS

In 1958, when the aluminum can was invented, steel had a monopoly on the soft-drink and beer-can market. People popped their cans with openers sometimes called "church keys." Aluminum had an advantage that proved irresistible to the beverage industry, however: a one-piece body that eliminated the unsightly and rust-prone side seam. And aluminum, being lighter, cut handling costs. Thirty years later aluminum had 95% of the soda-pop and beer-can business—but steel was preparing for a comeback. Technological advances have made tin-plated steel comparable to aluminum, the steel industry says. Steel now can be formed into a one-piece body, and steel has always had a price advantage over aluminum. Because it is a cheaper material, steel has neither the inherent value of aluminum nor the potential to become an environmental sweetheart through recycling programs. But it's easy to separate steel from trash with magnets.

Best way to get rid of steel (tin) cans: Recycle them in a curbside pickup program. This is the model being adopted in a number of communities that require separation of glass, metal, and paper. But simply tossing the can into mixed garbage is an equally responsible method if the trash stream is run through a resource recovery line.

Swimming Pool Chemicals

We once saw a demonstration of what can happen when certain pool chemicals are combined with innocent things like soft drinks, as might happen when both are compacted in a garbage truck. For a minute or two nothing happened, but then there was an explosive flare of fire and smoke. Don't try to replicate this chemical reaction—take our word for it.

Best way to get rid of swimming pool chemicals: In a household hazardous-waste collection program. Don't throw them in the trash.

TELEPHONE BOOKS

*B*efore plastic booster chairs were invented, kids were boosted on phone books—old directories boosted us to Grandma's table for numerous Thanksgivings. The phone company also used to pick up old books. Now, not only have they quit that practice ("It's so expensive to salvage them," a company representative says) but also we seem to be getting more directories all the time.

Phone books are tough to recycle—some people say there are no recognized markets. The paper is a very cheap grade of newsprint. The stickier problem, however, is the glue binding. It gums up the apparatus used to repulp paper, making phone books pariahs at paper mills. Removing the binding may cost more than the books are worth as scrap. Considering all these problems, some phone companies dispose of their excess quantities of directories—unused books still stacked on pallets from the printer—by shipping them directly overseas to places like Pakistan and Korea, where there is a demand for paper and labor is cheaper.

Best way to get rid of telephone books: Officials in two recycling trendsetting cities—Santa Monica, California, and Portland, Oregon—have found local buyers of scrap directories for phone-book roundups. The trick is to

estimate how many tons of books a collection campaign will bring in, get a buying commitment from a paper dealer, and collect the books—with free labor, if possible. Tell your local officials. Then you can toss your old books in the trash with a clear conscience.

THERMOMETERS, MERCURY TYPE

*T*his concerns medicine-cabinet thermometers. If one should break, a small amount of mercury may spill. It's important to collect as many of the droplets as you can, especially to avoid exposing toddlers and pets to the harmful mercury vapor. Your objective is to gather the droplets into one large drop, using a toothpick or piece of paper as a pusher. Don't use metal—the mercury will cling to it. And don't use a vacuum! That will only atomize the mercury and contaminate the appliance. Store the recovered drop of mercury in a tightly closed container.

Best way to get rid of a drop of mercury: Take it to your dentist's office. Dentists use mercury in fillings and recycle it regularly.

TIRES

*E*verybody knows what you do with an old tire—you hang it from a tree and make a swing! Too bad the number of old oaks isn't a better match for the mountains of worn-out radials. Currently the nation is wearing out 240 million tires a year—about one tire per person per year. But we are recycling only 40 million. What happens to the remaining 200 million? Though an unsightly number still are just dumped by the roadside, most are heaped onto growing stockpiles of tires awaiting some good second use. Tire-industry experts say there are two to three billion old tires stacked up on the national landscape.

Tires resist disposal in a unique way. Because of their shape, they trap air and other gases generated in a landfill. This buoyancy, plus the vibration of large equipment moving back and forth at the dumpsite, makes tires rise to the surface—they don't stay buried. Most dumps won't accept tires unless they are sliced in half like a bagel or chopped into small pieces. Even if your friendly garbage collector accepts your worn-out radials with the weekly trash, he'll probably have to find someplace other than the dump to get rid of them. Stacking old tires aboveground can lead to nasty problems. Again because of their shape, tires trap water and become breeding grounds for

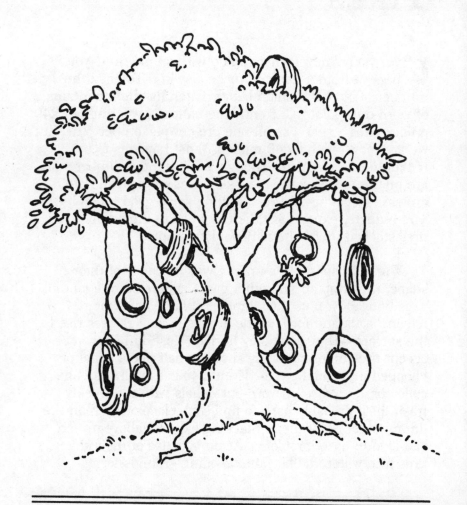

mosquitoes. A number of states have reported major fires in tire stockpiles—some have smoldered for months.

Despite bad press, old tires can be put to many good uses. Retreading is possible if they are not too far gone. Battered, bald tires can be strapped together and sunk offshore, making a reeflike feeding place for fish. Tires are used as dock dumpers and as shoreline erosion-control devices. Marine uses don't consume very many old tires, however. Larger volumes are going into reprocessing plants where tires are pulverized, combined with binder chemicals, and molded into new products. Much of this work is still in experimental stages. The most promising technique for retiring large volumes of the tire surplus is to burn tires whole, capture the heat to generate steam, and harness the steam in an electric turbine. Thus old tires become new kilowatts. The first U.S. plant of this kind is in the California foothills east of Modesto, next to what is believed to be the world's largest stockpile of tires—a cache of 40 million, enough to fuel the plant for ten years.

Best way to get rid of tires: Leave them in a dealer's custody. This assumes you are trading for new. But be wary: Unless you are firm about making an exchange, the "trade" of old tires may be a short circuit from your wheels into your trunk. The dealer has disposal problems too! If you are not trading old for new, the best idea is to put tires out for pickup by your garbage hauler. You may be charged a dollar or two extra, but you've done the right thing. The likelihood of turning an old tire into something useful and nonpolluting is much better when it's part of a regulated disposal system. The used-tire markets will spot the stockpiles a lot faster than tires thrown in the creek.

TELEVISION SETS

You are upgrading your image and have an old set to dispose of. Assuming it still works, the set will be welcomed in many group living quarters, such as nursing homes, colleges, prisons, and community shelters. A phone call should line up a user. Voluntary agencies that collect and resell household goods also like to receive TV sets in operating condition, and some even repair broken sets, though they don't like to broadcast the fact.

Best way to get rid of television sets: Give them to another user. For fast local disposal, place them at the curb with a FREE sign.

Toys

The trick in disposal of toys is to move them from your household to another household while the toys are still popular and serviceable. That way you both acquire space and perform a social good. The window for launching toys into such an orbit is very narrow. We have often waited too long and been stuck with armloads of plastic paraphernalia that no kid is interested in. But stuffed animals always seem to be negotiable.

Best way to get rid of toys: With consent of the owners, give them to another user to enjoy.

WEED KILLER

*R*ead instructions on the label. Also read "Insecticides," p. 70.

WINDSHIELD-WASHER FLUID

*B*est way to get rid of surplus windshield-washer fluid: Tie a red ribbon on the handle and present leftovers to another car owner. Driving where we do, we can't imagine ever having enough of this stuff. But if you can't even give it away, flush the liquid down the toilet. The empty container can be used to store dirty motor oil or paint solvents being held for a household hazardous-wastes collection.

WIRE COAT HANGERS

Wire coat hangers are simply packaging, like the plastic bag that covers laundry and dry cleaning. Yet they seem to defy disposal, multiplying on the closet rod until they become a nuisance. At our place, gangs of coat hangers are periodically split up and sent to hang out in remote corners of the household. They are incorrigible and inevitably must be thrown out, but not without a fight. They instantly turn an empty wastebasket full to overflowing. They catch other trash and poke the lid off the garbage can. They serve no purpose in a landfill and only melt into slag in an incinerator.

Better way to get rid of wire coat hangers: Start a trend—take them back to the dry cleaner for reuse. Most are in mint condition when tossed. And you might get a few cents off the bill.

WOOD see "Construction Debris," p. 43.

Z—Everything
That's Left

We have reached the end of the alphabet of household trash and there are quite a few leftovers. Toothpaste tubes, frozen juice cans, wax paper cartons, laundry soap boxes, microwave food containers, plastic "blister" packs—much of the unclaimed junk is product packaging. What's the best way to get rid of these things?

For most miscellaneous discards, there are just two options: burn or bury. The choices are limited because the leftovers, in general, are composite materials. Unlike aluminum cans or corrugated paper boxes or glass bottles —each made of a single material—composite containers are made of several. An example is a refrigerated tube of pastry dough, consisting of a paper cylinder with plastic inner liner, aluminum-foil outer layer, and steel end caps. Our nation's trash technology is not smart enough yet to economically salvage the separate ingredients in packages like that.

But rather than wait for technology to catch up at the trash end of the line, a better approach may be to ask what can be done at the production end to reduce the sheer volume of paper, metal, glass, plastic, foil, cardboard, and other materials flowing into the consumer system. That kind of thinking is called "source reduction," which many people believe is the best overall solution to the daily challenge of finding "The Best Way To Get Rid of Practically Everything Around the House."